THE WORLD OF
YOUR BUSINESS

PLAYBOOK

How to create a world of
welcome & belonging for you
and your customers

THE WORLD OF YOUR BUSINESS

PLAYBOOK

How to create a world of welcome & belonging for you and your customers

HIRO BOGA

DEVA PUBLISHING
LANTZVILLE • BC • CANADA

Cover and interior design: Calyx Design

Published by Deva Publishing, P.O. Box 94
Lantzville, BC V0R 2H0 Canada

HiroBoga.com

CONTENTS

FOREWORD

As I write this, I have just, for what I think is the 11th time so far, set aside the book you're looking at, and released a full-bodied exhale of gratitude. The questions in *The World of Your Business Playbook* have, like Hiro herself, become cherished friends – leaning close, speaking truth – and no matter how complex, random or elusive my ideas feel, neither of them has ever let me down.

I've been so blessed to experience how exceptional Hiro is as a teacher. Perhaps her most outstanding gift to us is her ability to show us what we know, inside. Like each of the chapters she's written, she gently but firmly turns my attention within, and through the power of the questions she asks, the noise of other people's opinions fades.

The worst possible thing when building a business, I like to say, is to spend an eon and a lot of resources to get your ducks in a row, and after all that effort, discover they aren't your ducks.

Being in Hiro's presence commands me to be faithful to my soul and leave other people's ducks alone. Working with this text, incredibly, does the same. Warm, well-loved, and filled with space for miracles, my copy is *The Velveteen Rabbit* (favourite children's book) of all of my business-building tools.

So, befriend the questions in each chapter, and be inspired and supported to be bolder than ever in your creations. If I've learned anything from Hiro, it's that your business wants you to be as you as possible.

Andrea J. Lee
CEO, Thought Partners International
March 2018

INTRODUCTION

**REMEMBER A TIME WHEN YOU WALKED INTO
A BUSINESS THAT FELT LIKE A SANCTUARY.**

Maybe it was a yoga studio, a theater, a bookstore, a spa, or a neighborhood café. Perhaps it was a virtual business – a website or blog that expanded your heart, lifted your spirits; that made you go "ahhhhh!"

As you entered the business, you felt embraced, welcomed and at ease. You may have felt a sense of spaciousness and possibility – an inner feeling that you could be all of yourself, here. A feeling of: *I'm home. I belong here.*

You felt at home in the world of that business.

It happened because someone took the time and care to design that business with love, to help you feel safe & welcome.

The lighting and ambience are warm and inviting, or elegantly zen; the aesthetic and design of the space, its offerings, the way you are greeted, your experience while you're there – every detail is thoughtfully created to be part of a harmonious whole, infused with grace.

It evokes in you the feelings that are at the heart of this business: Grace, elegance, safety, humor, playfulness, adventure, exploration, kindness, wit, love, generosity – all the soul qualities of the business, which are also qualities of your own soul, are expressed here. You feel them, as soon as you enter the world of this business.

You can create that experience of harmony, wholeness and belonging, for your clients & customers.

Your business is an eco-system, a *world*, with its own soul and essence, its own aesthetic, its own unique language and culture.

The World of Your Business Playbook is designed to help you map the world of your business – its culture, topography, language, customs and values. How it looks and feels, what purpose it serves, and how it serves the folks who live and visit there.

When you know the world of your business intimately, you can shape it consciously, and your clients and customers will know, right away, if they belong there.

This playbook is a living, evolving creation – a reflection of the growing world of your business. You can revisit it each year, each season, or at the start of each new project, to refine your thoughts and to reshape your world.

It's a big, deliciously nuanced document – with well over a hundred pages of questions to explore, in 14 chapters & playsheets.

It's an adventure in creative cartography ...

Every world needs a clear & compact guidebook, complete with maps, to help navigate it. Your business does too.

Enjoy the journey of articulating the origins, values, customs & economy of your business. Along the way, you'll create an invaluable blueprint for the unfolding, evolving world of your business.

ORIGINS

WHY DOES YOUR BUSINESS EXIST?
WHAT IS ITS REASON FOR BEING?

Your business has its own soul, its own purpose, and its own reason for being. It has its own life, its own world. Your customers are visitors in the world of your business.

Your privilege, as an entrepreneur, is to extend hospitality – to make them feel safe, welcome, and deeply held, from the moment they arrive.

Safe enough to connect with you, be with you, learn with you, and buy from you.

Safe enough to benefit from your work, come home to themselves as a result of it, and fully receive the blessings that your business offers.

Every world is created for a reason – and every world has its own essential qualities that make it both instantly recognizable, and utterly unique.

Because your customers and your business are living souls, they share all the essential qualities of soul. So, if the soul qualities of your business are clearly expressed, your customers will feel safe and welcome in the world of your business.

But, we have our being along a spectrum, from unity and essence to pattern and form. In its pattern and form, your business has essential qualities that are unique to it, just as your customers have qualities that make them uniquely themselves.

When customers recognize that your business's essential qualities – both on a soul level, and on the level of pattern and form – harmonize with their own, they feel: "I am here. I am home."

Soul qualities are not feelings – but you experience them through your feeling sense. Think about the last time you visited a new place, or met someone you'd never met before. You may not know the language or the geography of the place you're visiting, but you can feel its essential qualities. You may not know the person you've just been introduced to, but you have a felt sense of their presence, which is really a felt sense of their soul's qualities.

You might hear someone say:

> "Canada is such a beautiful country, with so much exquisite, pristine wilderness to explore! I can't wait to visit!"

Beauty, purity, exploration and adventure are among Canada's soul qualities. If those qualities resonate with your heart, you'll feel at home in Canada.

> "New York City is so culturally rich, diverse, & fast-paced! It feels frenetic and chaotic, but also exciting and fun. I'd like to visit for a week or two, but I don't think I'd want to live there."

Cultural richness and diversity, speed, creative chaos, fun are among New York City's essential qualities. Some of these translate into soul qualities of creativity, abundance, art, play, and flow. Others, like ambition, style, and momentum are qualities of the city's personality. Together, they form NYC's essential qualities. If that mix of qualities doesn't resonate strongly for you, you might not want to stay there, for long.

Q **What are the essential qualities that are at the heart of your business? Some of these will be soul qualities. Others will be qualities of the personhood of your business.**

Choose a few core qualities from the list below, add some of your own, or or explore my free online Deva Cards (hiroboga.com/deva-cards) for a more comprehensive list of soul qualities.

Action	Fun	Power
Adventure	Generosity	Sensuality
Abundance	Grace	Serenity
Buoyancy	Humor	Simplicity
Connection	Innovation	Spaciousness
Creativity	Intimacy	Strength
Curiosity	Kindness	Tenderness
Depth	Love	Transformation
Devotion	Mystery	Truth
Delight	Momentum	Wealth
Ease	Peace	Wholeness
Elegance	Prosperity	Wisdom
Friendship	Play	Wonder

Once you've identified the essential qualities of your business, it's much easier to articulate why your business exists – its purposes for being.

Like you, your business has a soul purpose – which is always about experiencing, expressing and serving soul qualities – as well as an incarnational purpose, which arises from its unique preferences, skills, genius and heart.

For example:

If two of your business's essential qualities are Celebration and Gratitude, then your business's soul purpose – which informs everything you offer through the world of your business – will be to be a beacon of celebration and gratitude in an often painfully competitive world.

If another of your business's essential qualities is Sensuality, then your business's incarnational purpose might be to serve in a very specific way – by offering products and services that celebrate the sacredness of the body and bring gratitude for the sensual beauty of the everyday world.

Q Why does the world of your business exist?

Try using these fill-in-the-blank prompts to get closer to your answer.

One of my business's essential soul qualities is ....

and my business's reason for being is to:

Another one of my business's essential soul qualities is ....

so my business serves as a reminder to:

One of my business's essential incarnational qualities is ....

and my business's reason for being is to:

Another one of my business's essential incarnational qualities is ....

so my business serves as a reminder to:

Since my business's essential qualities include .... &

.... , all of my products & offerings are designed to:

When people talk about my business, I want them to describe it as a place to feel

.... experience ....

and do:

If you want a life filled with .... & ....

then you belong in the world of my business.

Notes:

VALUES AND BELIEFS

**WHAT DO PEOPLE VALUE, BELIEVE & HOLD DEAR,
IN THE WORLD OF YOUR BUSINESS?**

Every human being has a set of values – operating principles for life, work & relationships. Tribes, cultures, cities, and nations have values, too.

For example:

The United States of America places a high value on individual freedom and democracy. If you value personal freedom, and the complex web of rights and responsibilities that accompany citizenship in a democratic society, then the USA will call to you.

Bhutan places a high value on happiness – they even track & measure it, nationally. If you want to explore the art & science of happiness, then you'll feel at home in Bhutan.

Ireland places a high value on the arts. Artists are given tax exemptions and a place of honor in Irish society. If you are a poet, playwright, writer or artist, you will feel supported and held, in Ireland.

Israel values lineage and faith. If you have Jewish ancestry, the government will fly you to Israel, free of charge, as part of their homecoming program. If you are Jewish, and want to explore your spiritual heritage, then you might feel called to the country of Israel.

As an entrepreneur, the more clearly articulate your business's values, the more readily your customers will know whether or not they belong in the world of your business. Those customers who belong with you will come to you, and those who don't, will go elsewhere. This makes for a harmonious business ecology, and good business relationships.

....

Q **What do you value, so deeply, that it forms the heart of your business? List each of your core values.**

In the world of my business, we value ....

In the world of my business, we value ....

In the world of my business, we value ....

Q **What are you willing to take a stand for? What principles do you live by — no matter what?**

In the world of my business, we stand for ....

Q **What are some of your deepest, most essential beliefs? List them.**

In the world of my business, we believe ....

In the world of my business, we believe ....

In the world of my business, we believe ....

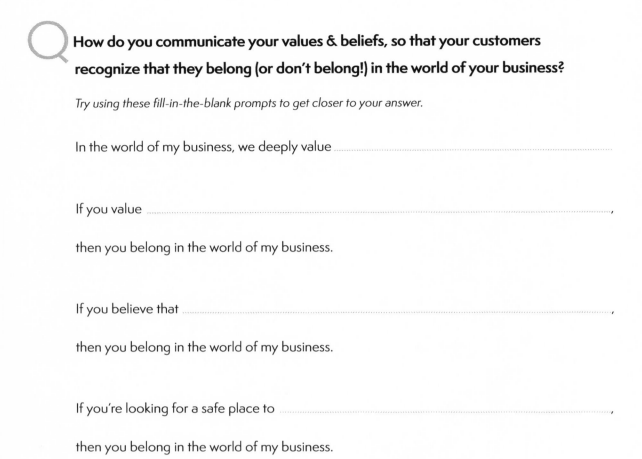

How do you communicate your values & beliefs, so that your customers recognize that they belong (or don't belong!) in the world of your business?

Try using these fill-in-the-blank prompts to get closer to your answer.

In the world of my business, we deeply value ....

If you value .... ,

then you belong in the world of my business.

If you believe that .... ,

then you belong in the world of my business.

If you're looking for a safe place to .... ,

then you belong in the world of my business.

Notes:

LANGUAGE

HOW DO PEOPLE COMMUNICATE, IN THE WORLD OF YOUR BUSINESS?

Every nation has a language & communication style, all its own.

To offer a few examples:

In California, communication tends to be laid back & informal. It's generally fine to use casual phrases ("hey," "dude," "wow!"). There's a sense of friendliness & warmth.

On the other hand, in corporate Japan, communication tends to be spare & precise, with a high value placed on the use of proper titles & honorifics.

The world of your business has a language, too – with its own vocabulary, tone, style, cadence and rhythm.

The language you use in your business is most powerful when it emerges from your deep presence, and reflects the way that you naturally think & speak.

If you try to sound like somebody else, you'll find it hard to connect with your customers. They'll feel the discrepancy between your natural voice and the one you've crafted for your sales page, blog, newsletter or other written material. This will leave them feeling uneasy, because your business's communication doesn't resonate with its presence. When you express yourself naturally, it helps your customers trust you – they feel safe in the world of your business.

How do people communicate, in the world of your business?

Try using these fill-in-the-blank prompts to get closer to your answer. Your responses to these writing prompts will vary, depending on the aspect of communication you're considering. For example, your sales page may use a slightly different style of communication than you would use when writing a newsletter to your list. And both of those will be different from the style you use when writing to a beloved colleague, or a long-time client.

The idea here is to articulate the general principles of how you communicate, so that your communication style is harmonious across the whole world of your business. This becomes particularly important when you have a number of people on your team. Each of your team members will have their unique voice, but when they all clearly understand the communication culture of your business, your customers' experience in the world of your business will be seamless and unified.

In the world of my business, we welcome visitors with ....

In the world of my business, we bid our visitors farewell by ....

In the world of my business, we help our visitors feel heard and understood by

....

In the world of my business, we never use words like ....

.... , or ....

In the world of my business, we strive to make every conversation and interaction feel like a

....

In the world of my business, we meet conflict or potential conflict by

....

Q How are your business's essential qualities, values & beliefs expressed, through your marketing language?

For example:

If one of your business's essential qualities is peace, then does every sales page, newsletter, and web page invoke a feeling of peace?

If one of your business's values is freedom, then your website copy might be an invitation to explore and choose your own path, or it might read like a revolutionary manifesto.

If one of your business's beliefs is that All beings are worthy of love and respect, then your next blog post might be written as a tender love letter.

One of my business's essential qualities is .... , so my

marketing language feels like ....

One of my business's values is .... , so my marketing

language feels like ....

One of my business's beliefs is .... , so my marketing

language feels like ....

Notes:

LINEAGE

WHO LAID THE FOUNDATIONS ON WHICH THE WORLD OF YOUR BUSINESS IS BUILT?

Your business did not spring up like a weed, from a seed that blew in on a random wind. It is grounded in the lives, generosity, and wisdom of its ancestral lineages.

Just as you have both a maternal and a paternal lineage, your business too has dual lineages.

Your business's spiritual lineage includes the wisdom traditions that anchor its values, and shape its vision, purpose, and way of being in the world. It includes those teachers and mentors who have walked the path before you, whose spiritual insights and devotion form the ground in which your business is rooted.

Your business's spiritual lineage also includes its Deva, and other allies in the subtle energy realms who contribute to its unfolding life and hold both its soul essence and the pattern for its perfect unfolding.

Your business also has a business lineage, which includes the industry or business tradition to which it belongs.

If your business is writing and publishing, for example, your business lineage includes the entire tradition of writing and publishing – from the early cuneiform writing of the Sumerians, to the Gutenberg press and the invention of movable type, to the artists who lent their skills to creating typography that's still in use today. to the technological geniuses who are creating the emerging frontiers of digital publishing.

Your business lineage also includes your own teachers – those from whom you have learned the skills, knowledge, cumulative experience and wisdom of your tradition. Once again, if we use the example of a writing and publishing business, your business lineage includes writers whose work inspires and informs your own, whether or not you've ever met them in person. It includes your fifth-grade grammar teacher, your poetry prof at college, and those writers and editors, book designers, typographers and publishers who have mentored you.

When customers step into the world of your business, they experience the foundation on which this world is built. Honor your business's lineages – both the practical tradition of craft or entrepreneurship, on which your business rests, and the spiritual and subtle energy beings whose wisdom and power add to its substance and strength.

Honoring your lineages creates grounding and safety for you and your customers. It reminds you that you are not alone – that the world of your business is built on the lives and contribution of others who have gone before you. It adds depth & credibility to your work. In showing your customers the origins of your business, you build trust.

Q Who are the people (living or dead, real or fictional) that have influenced your worldview?

Writers:

Wisdom Keepers:

Entrepreneurs:

Artists:

Researchers:

Teachers:

Employers:

Colleagues:

Family:

Friends:

Q **Who are the people who have helped to build the practical, everyday world of your business?**

Website designers:

Graphic designers:

Coaches:

Mentors:

Photographers:

Videographers:

Copywriters:

Editors:

Assistants:

Cheerleaders:

How are you currently honoring & expressing your lineage, in the world of your business?

For example:

Citing sources in articles.

Hyperlinking to blog posts that inspire my work.

Including my influencers in a Resources section of my website.

Thanking collaborators in a Gratitude section of my e-book.

Profiling or interviewing people who inspire me.

Q **Can you communicate your lineage to your customers, in a sentence or two?**

Try using these fill-in-the-blank prompts to get closer to your answer.

When I invite people into the world of my business, I am standing gratefully on the ground

prepared by those who have come before me, including:

....

When I invite people into the world of my business, I am standing joyfully next to my peers &

colleagues, including: ....

When I invite people into the world of my business, they will be influenced by those who have

influenced me, including: ....

Notes:

ENVIRONMENT

WHAT DOES IT FEEL LIKE TO VISIT THE
WORLD OF YOUR BUSINESS?

Think about the way you feel, when you stroll through an early morning farmers' market in your neighborhood.

You might breathe in the fresh tang of heirloom tomatoes & newly picked basil; stop to chat with a local farmer about his bumper crop of broad beans and purple broccoli; buy a vibrant bouquet of field flowers from a zinc bucket. You feel a sense of community, liveliness, and connection to the earth.

Now, imagine stepping into an upscale, gourmet food store.

As you browse the aisles, you discover exotic foods, & sparkling bottles of champagne. You might learn about oysters or cave-aged cheese from the store's resident epicure. You feel a sense of sophistication, luxury and (appealing) exclusivity.

Both places serve the same purpose: they sell food.

But the farmers' market and the upscale food store have dramatically different environments. They feel different. They are different worlds.

The world of your business has its own environment, too – an environment that you have the power to shape through your marketing language, business model, the citizens & visitors you invite into your world, and the offerings you lay on the table.

Q What kind of *environment* do you want to create for your clients & customers?

Try using these fill-in-the-blank prompts to get closer to your answer.

The entrance to my business is ....
(For example: Clearly marked, open and welcoming. Hidden, invisible, or difficult to get to.
Gated, private and exclusive.)

People will recognize the entrance to the world of my business when they see

....

When people first enter the world of my business – or visit my website, for the first time – I want

them to feel ....

Once they are inside the world of my business, people will encounter the following signposts

and pathways, to guide them through the world of my business.

....

As people explore the world of my business, they'll discover places where they

....

As people explore the world of my business, they'll meet ....

....

As people explore the world of my business, they'll be delighted and surprised by

....

My customers will love and appreciate the fact that my business environment includes

....

My customers will appreciate the fact that my business environment does not include

....

My business environment expresses my business's essential qualities, by

....

Notes:

Notes:

CITIZENS

WHO LIVES IN THE WORLD OF YOUR BUSINESS?

Every nation has citizens: people who live there, who help shape its economy and culture, and who participate fully in its everyday life.

Even if you are the only citizen in the world of your business, right now, soon, you may want to invite others to join you in creating a vibrant, healthy society.

For the world of your business to flourish, you'll use your discernment to choose the people you want to share it with, and you'll establish laws and guidelines to govern the society that you'll form together.

You'll want to seek out potential citizens who share your values & beliefs, speak the native language of your business, live in a way that is harmonious with the world of your business, and embody the essential qualities of your business.

Many nations have "skilled worker" policies – meaning, only people who contribute highly desirable & necessary skills are invited to become residents.

What kinds of skilled workers does the world of your business need, right now?

For example:

Writers	Photographers	Graphic designers
Editors	Videographers	Coaches and Consultants
Website designers	Copywriters	Administrative assistants
Project managers		

 How long do you want your skilled workers to stay, in the world of your business?

For example:

A year

Three months

For the duration of my next product launch

For the entire life of my business

How will you ensure that your skilled workers feel safe, supported, & welcome, in the world of your business?

For example:

I will provide them with two weeks of training from my assistant, project manager or other skilled support person.

I will be accessible for questions, during their first week.

I will enlist my business manager to help them get settled.

I will give them a copy of my business operations manual, or of this completed workbook, as a guide to values, customs, communication & operational style in the world of my business.

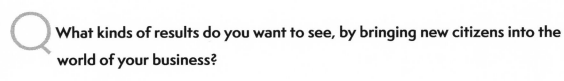 **What kinds of results do you want to see, by bringing new citizens into the world of your business?**

For example:

A measurable increase in newsletter subscribers.

A measurable increase in sales and/or net profits.

An effortless launch, without any technical glitches and with an enrollment of ....

A noticeable feeling of ease & spaciousness, as administrative and other tasks are skillfully handled.

A specific amount of liberated time in which I can create, innovate, and expand my business.

How will you celebrate your skilled workers' success, and encourage them to remain in the world of your business?

For example:

I'll offer a year-end bonus for exceptional contributions.

I'll offer my support as a friend & mentor, to support their own business growth.

I'll send gifts, flowers & handwritten love notes letting them know how much I appreciate them, and naming the ways in which they contribute to the world of my business.

I'll support their ongoing learning and professional growth.

Notes:

Notes:

VISITORS

WHO ARE THE CUSTOMERS WHO FLOW THROUGH THE WORLD OF YOUR BUSINESS?

Consider the way a city prepares for a major civic event – like hosting the Olympic Games, or welcoming a community of world leaders who are meeting to make decisions about global environmental or economic policies that will shape the future of the world.

The city will probably begin preparing for the event years in advance. Designing budgets. Developing new roads and constructing new public buildings, transit systems and other permanent infrastructure. Expanding airports and preparing to receive a massive influx of visitors through national borders. Creating signage, maps and brochures. Organizing public events at a variety of venues; predicting and programming traffic flow; training and deploying security personnel; building visitor information centers; organizing food supply chains; hiring and training venue staff, and so much more.

All of this is done to make the event as seamless, efficient and pleasurable as possible for the people who will be visiting the city, as participants, support staff, or spectators.

You can prepare the world of your business for new customers & clients in much the same way. But, in order to make their visit to your world truly wonderful and memorable, you have to understand who your visitors are – what they long for, expect, value, and are traveling long distances to experience. You have to know what they are afraid of, and what makes them feel safe, supported, welcomed and at home. You have to know what inspires them to dream, and what gives them the courage to act, to fulfill their dreams.

When you understand your visitors, you can meet them where they are. You can offer them what they need to feel safely held, and at home in the world of your business. You can create systems and structures, products, programs and invitations that support your customers in fulfilling their true desires. In doing so, you also create what your business needs to thrive, so it can continue to be a sustainable source of inspiration and nourishment for the people it serves.

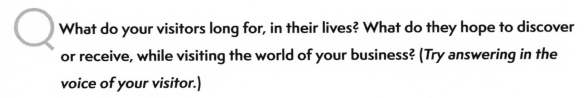

What do your visitors long for, in their lives? What do they hope to discover or receive, while visiting the world of your business? (*Try answering in the voice of your visitor.*)

For example:

Skills to help me know what I want, and tools to help me get from where I am to where I want to be.

Courage and faith to follow my own truth.

Tools to communicate more effectively, so I can express my needs and desires in a clear and sovereign manner, and have them met more easily.

Beautiful graphics that will enchant and bring in new customers.

Affirmation that my creative ideas are valuable and worth pursuing.

Technical and administrative support, so I can focus on my creative work.

Training and mentoring, so I can grow myself and my business more effectively.

Marketing support, so I can increase enrollment in my classes and programs.

Q **What are the values that are central to your visitors' sense of their own identity? What would they fight for, or even die for?** *(Again, try answering in the voice of your visitor.)*

For example:

To speak my truth freely and fearlessly.

To worship, pray, meditate and meet with my Creator in my own way.

To learn, grow, expand, and express my art.

To be loved, accepted, and appreciated for who I am and what I do.

To love and honor my creations.

To protect and provide for my family and the people I love.

To engage in creative work that emerges from my deep soul, makes a joyful contribution to my world, and brings me both prosperity and fulfillment.

To live in harmony with the natural world and with all of life.

To be responsible for my life and my choices, and to hold others accountable for theirs.

To contribute to a world that works for everyone.

What are some of the painful, fearful beliefs that your visitors hold about themselves, or their place in the world?

For example:

The world is a great, big, scary place, and I am all alone, in it. If I relax my vigilance, something terrible will happen.

Running a business is exhausting. I work all the time, but I'll never get ahead. There's always more to do.

There's something wrong with me. Life may be easy for other folks, but it can never be easy for me.

Nothing I do ever works out the way I had hoped, so what's the use in trying?

Good things don't last. The better things get, the more I have to watch out.
The backlash will come – it's only a matter of time.

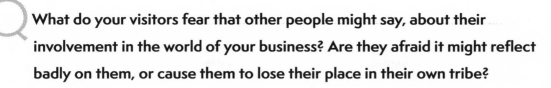

What do your visitors fear that other people might say, about their involvement in the world of your business? Are they afraid it might reflect badly on them, or cause them to lose their place in their own tribe?

For example:

I'm learning and growing so much, through this class, it feels really good – feels like coming home to myself. But, I'm worried my friends (or colleagues / family / boss) will think I'm weird or "woo-woo" for taking part in this.

This program is putting me in touch with my erotic, sensual self. I love it, but if my mother / partner / kids / dog knew I was doing this, they would be angry and punish me for it.

I love growing myself and my business in a truly organic way, using my discernment and intuition to guide me. But my partner thinks it's risky and unscientific, and I should stick with traditional marketing methods instead. I'm afraid he'll think I'm an irresponsible flake, if I don't do it his way.

I feel powerfully creative and alive, as I learn new ways of working. But I'm afraid my friends will be threatened by my success and will abandon me if I don't live down to their expectations.

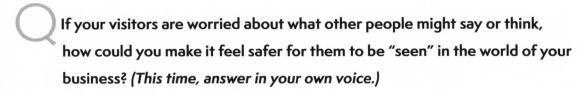 **If your visitors are worried about what other people might say or think, how could you make it feel safer for them to be "seen" in the world of your business?** *(This time, answer in your own voice.)*

For example:

I could invest in a beautiful, professional-looking website that is both welcoming and easy to navigate.

I could craft website copy that's thoughtfully sequenced, that walks new visitors through the world of my business in a way that's logically organized, fluid, clear and free of jargon.

I could write a thoughtful FAQ page that articulates their fears, allays their doubts, and gives them honest responsive answers to their questions.

I could provide sufficient information about my professional training, education and credentials to reassure them that they are in skilled hands.

I could seek out media opportunities to articulate my world-view and methodology, to provide social proof that my work is helpful & widely embraced.

I could include stories and testimonials from my clients, along with their photos and website urls, so my visitors can hear from others who have benefited from the world of my business.

Q **What are three practical things that you could do, right now, to create a safer, more welcoming world for your visitors?**

1.

2.

3.

Notes:

Notes:

ETHICS

HOW ARE PEOPLE TREATED, IN THE WORLD OF YOUR BUSINESS?

Every culture has its own moral standards and ethics – codes of conduct that clarify the culture's values and expectations, and establish how people are to behave, to ensure freedom, dignity, security and safety for everyone.

The world of your business has its own ethics, and codes of conduct.

Your business engages with people in a wide variety of ways. Clearly articulated rules of social conduct will help create a safe and welcoming environment for your customers and for you.

Perhaps you have a blog with open comments; online programs with a group forum to which people bring their deepest, most vulnerable selves; or live retreats where intensely personal stories are shared.

When you establish a clear and succinct code of conduct, everyone who enters the world of your business knows the rules of engagement in your world. This eases social relationships, makes it safe for people to open up and reveal themselves, knowing that their confidentiality will be protected and their creative ideas will be respected.

What is the code of conduct, in the world of your business?

Try using these fill-in-the-blank prompts as a starting point, as you outline your code of conduct.

In the world of my business, visitors are always treated with ....

In the world of my business, ... is never acceptable or tolerated.

In the world of my business, ... is always appreciated and rewarded.

In the world of my business, unhappy visitors are offered ....

In the world of my business, refunds may be offered in circumstances where

....

In the world of my business, refunds are *never* offered in circumstances where

....

In the world of my business, emails are answered within .... days.

In the world of my business, payment is expected ....

Q **Where and when is the code of conduct publicly articulated, in the world of your business?**

In the world of my business, my refund policy is clearly stated in ....

In the world of my business, my payment policies are detailed in ....

The code of conduct for my blog comments / participation in my classes, workshops and

retreats / private clients is explicitly stated in ....

I use .... to ensure that everyone who participates in the world

of my business understands and agrees with its code of conduct.

If someone deliberately transgresses against my business's code of conduct, my policy is

....

If someone inadvertently breaks the rules of social conduct in the world of my business, we

....

Notes:

Notes:

CUSTOMS

WHAT ARE THE UNIQUE CEREMONIES & CUSTOMS, IN THE WORLD OF YOUR BUSINESS?

Travel to Taipei on the fifteenth day of the first month of the lunisolar year, and you will see thousands of lanterns being released into the sky. Miraculous!

It's the Shangyuan Festival – an annual Chinese tradition dating back to the 6th century. Citizens prepare for this festival. Visitors arrive from around the world to witness it. Everyone celebrates.

Whether the world of your business is relatively new, or has a long and venerable history, you have the privilege of shaping its customs & ceremonies. And, you can introduce new traditions whenever you wish.

Q **What are the unique ceremonies & customs, in the world of your business?**

Try using these fill-in-the-blank prompts as a starting point.

My place of business has an altar dedicated to my business, which consists of

.... and where we ....

We begin each day in the world of my business, with ....

We end each day in the world of my business, with ....

We celebrate the beginning and end of each season in the world of my business with

....

We celebrate significant milestones in the world of my business, by ....

....

The major holidays in the world of my business are ....

and we celebrate them by ....

Every day in the world of my business, visitors can expect ....

Every week in the world of my business, visitors will enjoy ....

Every month in the world of my business, visitors can anticipate ....

....

In the world of my business, we contribute to our community by ....

....

In the world of my business, we celebrate birthdays & anniversaries by ....

....

One new tradition that I intend to introduce into the world of my business is ....

....

One outworn tradition that I am ready to relinquish now is ....

....

Notes:

Notes:

AESTHETICS

**WHAT DOES THE WORLD OF YOUR BUSINESS
LOOK LIKE — AND WHY?**

Beauty is a personal experience – a relationship between you and the world around you, shaped by your individual tastes and preferences, cultural conditioning and expectations, and inner sense of harmony. There is no universal definition of beauty – in art or design, in cityscapes, business or life.

You might find the neon hum & compressed vitality of downtown Manhattan utterly captivating, while someone else might find it overwhelming.

Yet while our individual definitions of beauty may differ, there are certain aesthetic features that emerge from our evolution as a species, and speak universally to the human heart.

Clean, horizontal lines. Open spaces. Curved horizons.

Harmony. Proportion. Balance.

Chiaroscuro. Contrast. Creative surprise.

The symmetry of stars.

Just as every nation, state or city is beautiful in its own way, the world of your business is uniquely beautiful too. As its creator, you get to choose how it will look and feel – and what response it will evoke in you, and in your visitors.

What is your personal definition of beauty?

Try using these fill-in-the-blank prompts as a starting point.

The beauty that takes my breath away is ....

I love beautiful ....

In the presence of exquisite beauty, I feel ....

For me, beauty is ....

For me, the opposite of beauty is ....

The places I love most are beautiful because ....

Beauty brings me closer to ....

Beauty brings my visitors & customers closer to ....

I want the world of my business to feel beautiful, so that my visitors will feel

....

Q **How can you carry your personal definition of beauty into the world of your business?**

I can make my website (or forthcoming website) more beautiful by ....

....

I can make my newsletter more beautiful by ....

I can make my writing, videos, podcasts, ebooks – and everything I produce – more

beautiful by ....

I can make my customer experience more beautiful by ....

I can make my business's physical home more beautiful by ....

I can make running my business feel more beautiful by ....

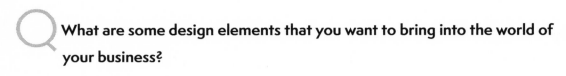

What are some design elements that you want to bring into the world of your business?

For example:

A color palette that invokes the fresh, variegated breath of spring.

Clean, open space, black and white palette, sans serif fonts, for a modern, minimalist aesthetic.

Angles and curvilinear shapes juxtaposed together, polyphony, chiaroscuro, to convey mystery, contrapuntal harmony, creative surprise.

Playful colors and shapes, images and textures, to invoke a feeling of buoyancy and fun.

Elegant fonts, lots of white space, muted color palette, for a classic look and feel.

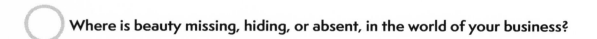

Where is beauty missing, hiding, or absent, in the world of your business?

Q In what regions of your business is hidden beauty aching to be revealed? What concrete steps can you take, to unveil it, today? In thirty days? In the next three months?

Notes:

Notes:

ENTRY & COMPLETION, SEQUENCING & NAVIGATION

HOW DO PEOPLE ENTER, MOVE AROUND IN, AND LEAVE THE WORLD OF YOUR BUSINESS?

Imagine that you wake up from a mid-day nap, and find yourself in the center of a crowded town square.

Vendors call out their wares, offering flowers, fruits & vegetables from wheeled carts. People stroll by, arm in arm, conversing intimately, or chatting and laughing in raucous groups. Street musicians play guitars and fiddles, strum banjos and beat out rhythms on hand-drums. One passes a blue top-hat around a circle of onlookers, and people drop in silver coins, a few crumpled notes. In the distance, a clock tower chimes – signaling that it's time for a grand event to begin.

It's exciting, it's energizing – but you have no idea how you got here.

You're in a place you've never seen before. You don't know the culture, the language, or if the natives are friendly. Above all, you don't know how you landed here. One minute, you were in your own bed. Next minute, here you are, in a town square with a party about to begin.

Your breathing becomes shallow. You freeze in place, confused and overwhelmed. You scan the crowd for an opening through which you can escape and find your way back to the safety of your own room, in your own home.

If the world of your business doesn't have a clearly defined entry – an arch or open gateway – and a well-lit and well-marked path from there to center of town, your visitors are likely to feel confused and lost. They won't know where they are, what's being offered, and where to go or what to do next.

By calling on the spirit of hospitality and empathy, and blending it with some thoughtful planning and preparation, you can create a clearly visible, welcoming entry into the world of your business.

Once your visitors have walked through the front gate, you can provide them with a well-marked and clearly lit pathway to guide them into the center of your town square. You can offer them maps and a guidebook, so that they arrive feeling welcomed, secure about what to expect and what is likely to happen next, and happy to join in the festivities!

What is the "town square" in the world of your business?

In other words: what is the central offering, product or experience that you want to guide your visitors towards?

The "town square" in the world of my business is ....

What is the "entry sequence" for the world of your business?

In other words: how will visitors know where to enter the world of your business? And what guides them from the boundary into the center of your town square?

When visitors arrive in the world of my business, the very first thing they'll see or experience is

....

When visitors arrive in the world of my business, the very first thing they'll be encouraged to

do is ....

Next, they'll be invited to .... , which will help them

feel safe & happy to ....

On their way to the town square, visitors will enjoy attractions, like ....

....

They'll know that they've arrived in the town square, because ....

....

Once they are in the town square, they'll be invited to ....

....

What is the "completion sequence" in the world of your business?

In other words, how do you honor and mark your customers' departure from specific areas or regions, in the world of your business?

When visitors have completed a private program, we celebrate by ....

....

When visitors have completed a group program, workshop, retreat, or other event, we mark

the occasion by ....

One or two weeks after visitors have completed a private or group program with me, they will

receive ....

Some examples:

A hand-written note thanking them for their participation.

An autoresponder, asking them how they are doing, with a link to a feedback form and an invitation to share their experience.

A gift, with a hand-written card.

A personal, follow-up email.

Notes:

ECONOMY

**HOW IS MONEY EXCHANGED IN THE WORLD
OF YOUR BUSINESS – AND FOR WHAT?**

Hawaii's economy is anchored by tourism, agriculture, aquaculture, and mining.

California's economy is fueled by technology and education, transportation, agriculture and entertainment.

British Columbia's economy is grounded in service industries, natural resources, and tourism.

The world of your business has its own unique economy, too.

It is comprised of valuable goods & services that can't be replicated by anyone else, anywhere else.

Most nations (and businesses) have two or three "leading exports" for which they are widely known.

This doesn't mean that you have to limit your business to two or three products or services. It does mean that your economy will be most vibrant if you focus on serving a particular population through clearly delineated areas of service which can comfortably hold all of your offerings.

Carving out boundaries in this way creates clarity and specificity. It lets your visitors know whom you serve, what needs and desires you fulfill, what they can expect from participating in the world of your business, and what you offer them that no-one else does. This makes it much easier for visitors to discern if they belong in the world of your business.

Before you decide what your exports are going to be, how much you will charge for them, and how they'll be distributed, take some time to consider these fundamental questions:

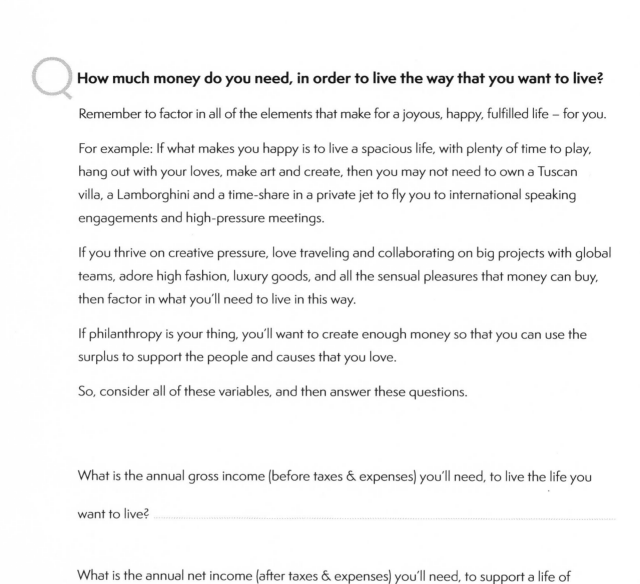

How much money do you need, in order to live the way that you want to live?

Remember to factor in all of the elements that make for a joyous, happy, fulfilled life – for you.

For example: If what makes you happy is to live a spacious life, with plenty of time to play, hang out with your loves, make art and create, then you may not need to own a Tuscan villa, a Lamborghini and a time-share in a private jet to fly you to international speaking engagements and high-pressure meetings.

If you thrive on creative pressure, love traveling and collaborating on big projects with global teams, adore high fashion, luxury goods, and all the sensual pleasures that money can buy, then factor in what you'll need to live in this way.

If philanthropy is your thing, you'll want to create enough money so that you can use the surplus to support the people and causes that you love.

So, consider all of these variables, and then answer these questions.

What is the annual gross income (before taxes & expenses) you'll need, to live the life you want to live? ....

What is the annual net income (after taxes & expenses) you'll need, to support a life of contentment and joy? ....

Once you've arrived at gross and net income numbers that feel right to you, use the worksheet at the end of this section to work out the mix, quantity and price of the products or services you'll have to sell, to make this income.

Q What are your current exports?

List all of your products, services, offerings & experiences. (Including free articles, videos, resources and gifts, if these are part of your world.)

Export No. 1:

This export is currently priced at ....

This export is highly valuable to visitors because:

This export is a beautiful reflection of the soul of my business because:

This export will be available in the marketplace until ....

Export No. 2:

This export is currently priced at ....

This export is highly valuable to visitors because:

This export is a beautiful reflection of the soul of my business because:

This export will be available in the marketplace until ....

Export No. 3:

This export is currently priced at ....

This export is highly valuable to visitors because:

This export is a beautiful reflection of the soul of my business because:

This export will be available in the marketplace until ....

Repeat this exercise, until you've described all of your exports.

 **Looking at your list of exports, ask yourself ...**

Do any of my exports feel as though they don't belong in the world of my business?

Do any of my exports feel underpriced? Why?

Do any of my exports feel overpriced? Why?

Are there any exports that are ready to be retired?

What are the leading exports that I want my business to be known for?

Has my best & most powerful export already been created, or is it still to come?

How is money exchanged in the world of your business?

Describe all of the ways that you accept payment for your exports. (For example: cash, check, credit card, PayPal, bank transfer.)

Do you have any "trade agreements" in place?

For example:

Payment for my exports is due upfront / upon receipt of invoice / within 30 days /

....

I'll consider bartering my exports for other valuable items, but only when ....

....

I do / do not offer a money-back guarantee, and my reasoning for that is ....

....

Q **How much money are your exports currently bringing in?**

Total before expenses:

(Minus expenses):

Total after expenses:

Q **How much money would you like your exports to bring in?**

Total before expenses:

(Minus expenses):

Total after expenses:

Q What needs to shift in the world of your business in order to meet your economic goals?

Q What is one practical thing you could do, right now, to encourage that shift to happen?

Now: let's bring all the economic pieces together in a simple chart.

This template is simply a place to start. You can photocopy it and re-use it, expand it, add other columns to it – customize it to fit your particular business.

Type of offering _For example: coaching program, workshop, book_	Number of offerings / year _For example: 12 clients/year, 4 workshops/year with 25 participants each, 1,000 books sold/year_	Revenue per participant / copy sold _Before taxes & expenses_	Cost per participant / copy, plus expenses & taxes	Total net income for offering type
Total income / year				

Notes:

Notes:

GROSS NATIONAL HAPPINESS

**WHAT DOES IT MEAN TO BE HAPPY,
IN THE WORLD OF YOUR BUSINESS?**

In the nation of Bhutan, "happiness," "satisfaction" and "quality of life" are measured just like population levels, imports and exports.

And each year, the government conducts a study analyzing Gross National Happiness (GNH), and publishes the results.

Bhutan's leaders maintain that measuring Gross National Happiness is just as important as measuring Gross National Product.

Imagine if every country on earth considered happiness as a measure of national success!

It might seem self-indulgent, or a pipe-dream, to think of happiness as a measure of success, when you are pouring all of your time, energy and resources into growing your business.

But happy people are creative, resilient, magnetic, and fun to be around. Truth is, unhappiness is just plain inefficient. Unhappy people are less productive, more anxious, more stressed, more tightly clenched, less able to respond to the needs of their markets. Unhappiness leads to ill health, lost time, missed opportunities, apathy, and uninspired offerings.

As we move towards the end of this workbook, spend some time considering what happiness means for you – and how you can build the world of your business to support and build happiness into the culture of your business.

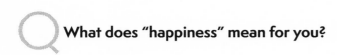 **What does "happiness" mean for you?**

The happiest time of my day is:

The happiest experiences of running my business are:

My happiness depends on:

My happiness does not depend on:

When I am happy, visitors & customers to the world of my business benefit because:

Q What is the *Gross National Happiness* for the world of your business?

In Bhutan, Gross National Happiness is measured in seven different areas of wellness.
Think of the following questions as an informal poll to measure your GNH.

Economic wellness

How satisfied are you with the quality of your exports?

How satisfied are you with the amount of money your exports are bringing in, after expenses?

How satisfied are you with your current pricing structure?

How satisfied are you with your current accounting & tax preparation systems?

How many visitors have ignored your invoices, requested refunds – or contested your pricing, in some way?

What would improve the economic wellness of your business?

Environmental wellness

How satisfied are you with your online environment? (Your website, blog or digital presence?)

How satisfied are you with your offline environment? (Your office, workspace, or brick & mortar business?)

What would improve the environmental wellness of your business?

Physical wellness

How do you feel about your physical body?

How often do you move & stretch, during your workday?

Are there any chronic issues (including stress-related issues) that are impeding your happiness or productivity?

What would improve your physical wellness?

Mental wellness

Out of every ten thoughts that pass through your mind ...

How many are positive & encouraging?

How many are negative & critical?

How many are neutral & observational?

Do you feel like the inside of your mind is a happy & safe place to be?

How satisfied are you with your ability to focus on projects?

How satisfied are you with your memory?

How satisfied are you with your emotional resilience, after a business set-back?

What would improve your mental wellness?

Workplace wellness

How satisfied are you with your workplace – your office, desk, or wherever you work most often?

How is the lighting? Temperature? Décor? Ambient noise?

How satisfied are you with your day-to-day rhythm, as you work?

If there are collaborators or co-workers sharing your workplace, how do you feel about sharing a space with them?

What would improve your workplace wellness?

Social wellness

How satisfied are you with the relationships you have in the world of your business?

Devas & other subtle energy beings:

Collaborators & Partners:

Colleagues & Friends:

Mentors:

Employees & Support Staff:

Clients & Customers:

Cheerleaders:

Which of your relationships feel the most nourishing?

Which feel the most draining or misaligned?

Which feel non-existent?

How satisfied are you with your visibility – your sense of "belonging" and "place" within the wider community?

How satisfied are you with your non-business relationships: friends, family, children, other loves?

What would improve your social wellness?

Political wellness

How satisfied are you with the leadership in the world of your business?
(Unless someone has recently usurped your position, that leader is you!)

If you were writing a letter to the leader of your business – like a citizen writing to the president or prime minister – what would you tell her?

If the role of sovereign leader was up for re-election, would you vote for yourself?
If you work with a team, how satisfied are you with the division of power, roles &

responsibilities in the world of your business?

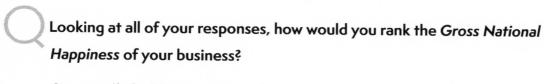

Q Looking at all of your responses, how would you rank the *Gross National Happiness* of your business?

Give yourself a fair & honest score, out of 100.

Q Which GNH area needs the most love & attention?

Circle one or two:

Economic wellness   Environmental wellness   Political wellness

Physical wellness   Mental wellness   Workplace wellness

Social wellness

Q What is one practical adjustment you could make to improve each of these areas? Right away? In the next three to six months?

Notes:

PROJECTS

**HOW ARE PROJECTS PLANNED & CARRIED OUT
IN THE WORLD OF YOUR BUSINESS?**

Every day, nations around the world undertake large-scale projects.

Sometimes, these projects are intended to create new exports, reduce spending & waste, or attract affluent tourists to the country. But often, national projects have nothing to do with cash flow – at least not directly.

Similarly, in the world of your business, "completing a project" doesn't necessarily mean "launching a product."

Your next project might be an aesthetic project – something to upgrade the look & feel of your business. It might be a structural project – something to improve the "entry sequence" for visitors, or the systems and structures that form the boundaries of your business's world. It might even be a cultural project – something to clarify your community code of conduct, or spark a new weekly tradition on your blog.

No matter what kind of project you choose, you will need a plan, a timeline, and a clear sense of what "completion" will mean for you.

The following questions might help you to create a flexible project plan – no matter what type of project you're planning!

Q What is your project's title & purpose?

The title of my project is ....

This project matters because ....

Q What is your project timeline?

I will begin working on my project on ....

I will complete my project on ....

I will know my project is complete when ....

(If publicizing this project is part of the plan) I will announce my project on

....

(If publicizing this project is part of the plan) I will promote my project from

.... to ....

Q **How will you measure your project's success?**

I will know my project is a success when ....

This project will help my visitors & customers to ....

This project brings more .... into the world of my business.

If publicizing your project is part of the plan, how will you draw attention to your project?

I will promote my project by ...

Connecting with past clients through a personal email or phone call.

Creating a series of blog posts.

Giving away a "teaser" or "sneak peek."

Holding a contest.

Hosting a preview class.

Inviting my allies & friends to help me promote it.

Pitching myself as a guest writer or speaker.

Privately inviting a handful of people to participate.

Purchasing advertisements.

Recording a promotional video.

Sending out a personal message to my readers.

Sending out a press release to local media.

Sending out postcards, flyers, or hard-copy marketing materials.

Talking about it on my social media channels.

Posting excerpts on social media channels.

Throwing a Twitter party.

Creating a Facebook event page.

Throwing a launch party.

Write down additional ideas, here:

What forms of support will you need to complete your project?

Think through each step of your project: planning / preparation / announcement / promotion / closure / celebration.

Website designers:

Graphic designers:

Coaches:

Consultants:

Photographers:

Videographers:

Copywriters:

Editors:

Assistants:

Cheerleaders:

Tools, spaces & supplies:

Both virtual & physical. For example:

An online shopping cart

A venue in my neighborhood

A space to upload & download video files

A program to design an e-book

Packing boxes & labels

Q How much *time* are you willing to invest in this project?

Q How much *money* are you willing to invest in this project?

Q How could you make the whole process *simpler* & *easier*?

Q How will you *celebrate* when it's complete? (Hooray!)

Now: let's bring all the project planning pieces together in a simple chart.

You'll begin with an overall description & timeline for a single project, and then create a breakdown of the various tasks that will need to be completed. You can photocopy this chart and use it for each of your projects. Feel free to refine it, add to it and tailor it to meet your own needs.

Project name	
Project purpose	
Start date	
End date	

Project task	Person responsible	Reporting to	Due date	Completed?

Notes:

Notes:

GROW YOUR BUSINESS.
GROW YOURSELF.

You've arrived at the end of this book. So ... what's next?

Whether your business is just finding its place in the world, or is a mature and powerful presence, it is an ever-evolving being. And so are you.

You grow your business by growing yourself.

Growth doesn't necessarily mean expansion. You grow in depth as well as height. When you cultivate spaciousness and depth in your inner world, your outer world expands and flourishes as well.

We are evolutionary beings, on a creative journey through life. To grow yourself, you grow your soul's presence. You grow your capacity to lead, innovate, and take creative risks; embody what you deeply love; and make friends with increasingly complex ecologies of relationship with the world around you.

To grow your business, you shape it to hold greater power, abundance, service, contribution and success; and more collaborative, complex relationships through which your business can evolve.

If you're ready to grow yourself and your business in this way, I'd be honored to accompany you on your journey.

Here are three places to begin:

RULE YOUR WORLD FROM THE INSIDE OUT
Sovereignty & the Art of Soul Leadership

Develop creative sovereignty in your life, and establish a strong foundation for your work, relationships and business.

This self-study program will give you a toolkit of energy technologies and skills with which to grow into the powerful ruler of your inner kingdom. In the process, your outer world will align with your inner vision in seemingly miraculous ways.

Learn more here:

hiroboga.com/rule-your-world

BECOME YOUR OWN BUSINESS ADVISER
Energy Alchemy for Creative Entrepreneurs

My signature, self-study business-building program, *Become Your Own Business Adviser* blends energy alchemy skills with refined business practices to help you shape your business in harmony with its inner being. Build a vibrant, prosperous, sustainable business that nourishes your heart, serves your community, and supports the life that you want to live.

You'll tap into your deep well of creative genius, bringing all of its powers into alignment for a very special purpose: to expand & evolve your business.

Learn more here:

hiroboga.com/become-your-own-business-adviser

DREAMING IN THE DARK
Craft the New Story of Your Business for The Year Ahead

Dreaming in the Dark is designed to be an at-home retreat. You'll receive everything you need to step out of the busy current of your life for two, nourishing days. You'll reflect, review, and release what no longer serves you. And you'll dream, envision, and create a vibrant new story for your business's future.

Learn more here:

hiroboga.com/dreaming-in-the-dark

· ·

Explore and enjoy these offerings – as well as my library of free resources (hiroboga.com/free-resources) & writings (hiroboga.com/blog).

May they support you in your perfect unfolding.

Love,

Hiro

ACKNOWLEDGEMENTS

Every book, and every business, is a collaborative creation. It owes its life, its vibrancy and health to everyone in its ecology. My business and I have an inner circle of allies – soul friends, soul family – whose genius and skill, support, generosity and love nourish me, and are the ground on which the world of my business is built.

I'm grateful to Richard Miller for his impeccable artistry in designing this book. Profound gratitude to Mandy McIlwraith for managing this project with skill and heart. A deep bow of thanks to beloved friends Jen Louden, Andrea Lee, Danielle LaPorte, and Alex Franzen for their loving support, and for offering their hearts, skills, and presence to help shape a soul-fuelled, radiant world. And to those of you who are reading this, thank you for bringing your own soul and genius to the making of our world.

Hiro Boga is a writer, master teacher and mentor to visionary leaders who are shaping a world in which service and prosperity, soul and entrepreneurship, work hand in hand to create a world that serves all of life.

Over the past thirty-five years, Hiro has helped thousands of clients and students reclaim joy, freedom, creative power and sovereignty in their businesses, their relationships, and their lives.

As a mentor and teacher, Hiro blends transformative energy technologies, the magic of story, and grounded spiritual practices with pragmatic business strategies.

Hiro offers a core curriculum of self-study programs in creative sovereignty, energy alchemy and soul-centered business. She works privately with evolutionary leaders to bring their most creative visions to life through a skillful blend of inner and outer work. The results are both practical and profound.

Explore her writing, sign up for her free 7-day e-course, *Sweet Success and the Soul of Your Business*, and discover a wealth of other resources at HiroBoga.com. Connect with her on Facebook and Instagram for daily doses of inspiration.

Made in the USA
Las Vegas, NV
09 November 2021